I LOVE
MY
MUM

Also published by Macmillan Children's Books

I LOVE MY MUM

Poems chosen by Gaby Morgan

Illustrated by Jane Eccles

MACMILLAN CHILDREN'S BOOKS

First published 2006 by Macmillan Children's Books
a division of Macmillan Publishers Limited
20 New Wharf Road, London N1 9RR
Basingstoke and Oxford
Associated companies throughout the world
www.panmacmillan.com

ISBN 978-0-330-44102-5

5 7 9 8 6 4

A CIP catalogue record for this book
is available from the British Library.

Printed and bound in the UK by CPI Mackays, Chatham ME5 8TD

*For my sensational mummy, Sue Morgan,
and scrumptious daughter, Evie Weston,
lots of love, Gaby*

*For the best mum ever, Zita Eccles,
with love from Jane*

Contents

Mother's Day

Mothering Sunday
should be a
mothering fun day.

Yes, where children should
smother their mother
with thanks and cuddles
for all those
pranks and muddles
she's had to deal with
throughout the year.

So let's hear it for all mums
with one great big
cheer!

Ian Souter

Spell to Make
Mum Smile

Say, Good morning Mum

You look particularly

pretty. How about

A nice cup of tea?

Roger Stevens

Things I Wish My Mother Would Not Do

Kiss me at the school gates – in front of all my
    friends
Tuck my shirt right down my pants – in front
    of all my friends
Clean my face with lick and spit – in front
    of all my friends
Give my dad a great big snog – in front
    of all my friends

Do anything at all – in front of all my friends!

Paul Cookson

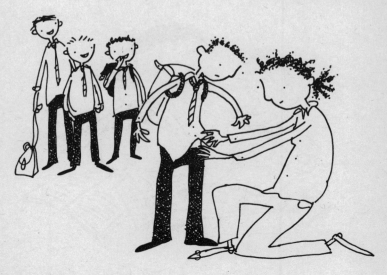

Mum is . . .

Rule maker
Side taker
Meal provider
Bedroom tidier
Game player
Bug slayer
Best carer
Love sharer
Tear drier
Treat buyer
Story teller
Homework helper

Peace keeper
Light sleeper
Money lender
Chief defender
However wild
Loves her child!

Catharine Boddy

A Card for Mum on Mother's Day

I love your curries,
Your chilli con carne,

The way you make
A tuna sarnie,

Your roast potatoes,
Yorkshire pud,

And crispy chips
Are good, good, good.

And I love it when you bake
A Very Special Birthday Cake.

I love your puddings,
Especially rice

With grated nutmeg . . .
Very nice!

Your mushy peas I love,
Your Irish stew,

But most of all, Mum,
I love YOU!

Matt Simpson

To Mother

Only she can tell the greatest story ever told
And kiss my forehead with the slightest touch
Make perfect pancakes, hold my hand to
cross the road
For all of this, I love her very much!

And she is one smart cookie, she can always
mend
Old dress buttons AND a broken heart
Hold me close and tell me, 'So you didn't win,
What matters only is the taking part.'

Most times she's more old-fashioned than
your grandma
She thinks the 70s always are in vogue
The men I date will never fit her bill
She thinks they're all unkempt ill-mannered
'rogues'!

She is the maddest monster, when she's angry
Her flying temper will take you by storm
And yet I know that she's a living legend
Of a breed exquisite, that is MOM.

Nicole Braganza

My Mum's put me on the transfer list

On Offer:
one nippy striker, eight years old
has scored seven goals this season
has nifty footwork and a big smile
knows how to dive in the penalty box
can get filthy and muddy within two minutes
guaranteed to wreck his kit each week
this is a FREE TRANSFER
but he comes with running expenses
weeks of washing shirts and shorts

socks and vests, a pair of trainers
needs to scoff huge amounts
of chips and burgers, beans and apples
pop and cola, crisps and oranges
endless packets of chewing gum.
This offer open until the end of the season
I'll have him back then
at least until the cricket starts.
Any takers?

David Harmer

New Rules

School gates
Gang of mates
Itching for you to play.

Your 'Bye'.
Eye to eye.
My first 'Don't kiss me!' day.

Sue Cowling

Surfing
(For Sam)

You storm the placid seas in a battleship,
waste depth charges on sand dunes,
fire your cannons at little fish,
turn ripples into waves.

You complain of boredom in the straits,
set full steam ahead from safe harbour,
pit your strength against the tide,
capsize your boat in deep waters.

While I, who taught you how to swim the
    shallows,
surf the breakers of my heart
to collect the debris.

June English

Every Day in Every Way

I see you
Every day
I love you
In every way
You help me
Every day
You love me
In every way,
Mother.

I cherish you
Every day
I need you
In every way
You cherish me
Every day
You need me
In every way,
Mother.

Devon Conrad (11)

Crazy Mayonnaisy Mum

When my friends come home with me
They never want to stay for tea
Because of Mum's peculiar meals
Like strawberries with jellied eels.
You should see her lick her lips
And sprinkle sugar on the chips,
Then pass a cup of tea to you
And ask, 'One salt or two?'

Whoops-a-daisy
That's my crazy
Mayonnaisy mum.

She serves ice cream with baked beans,
And golden syrup with sardines,
And curried chocolate mousse on toast,
And once she iced the Sunday roast.
When my birthday comes she'll make
A steak and kidney birthday cake.
There'll be jelly too, of course,
With cheese and onion sauce.

Whoops-a-daisy
That's my crazy
Mayonnaisy mum.

What's she put in my packed lunch?
A bag of rhubarb crisps to crunch.
Lots of sandwiches as well,
But what is in them? Who can tell?
It tastes like marmalade and ham,
Or maybe fish paste mixed with jam.
What's inside my flask today?
Spinach squash – hooray!

Whoops-a-daisy
That's my crazy
Mayonnaisy mum.

Julia Donaldson

Mothers

Some call mothers 'Mum'.
Some say 'Mummy' or 'Ma'.
Whatever you call yours,
She deserves a big gold star!

John Kitching

Just Mum and Me

We didn't do anything special today,
just mum and me.
Raining outside, nowhere to go,
just mum and me.

So we baked and talked and talked and baked
and baked and talked,
just mum and me.

She told me about when she was young
and how her gran baked exactly the same cakes
on rainy days and baked and talked to her.

She remembered her friends and the games
    they used to play,
the trees they used to climb,
the blackberries they picked,
the fields they used to run around in
and how summers always seemed to be sunny.

And mum smiled a smile I don't often see,
the years falling away from her face
and, just for a moment,
I caught a glimpse of the girl she used to be.

We didn't do anything special today,
raining outside, nowhere to go,
so we baked and talked and talked and baked,
just mum and me.

I ate and listened and listened and ate,
the hours racing by so quickly.

We didn't do anything special . . .
but it was special, really special.

Just mum and me.

Paul Cookson

My Mum's Speedy Day

My mum
Leaps out of bed,
Flips through the paper,
Flies round with the vacuum,

Dashes off a letter,
Nips to the loo,
Pops to the shops,

Runs slap bang into friends,
Races home,
Grabs a bite to eat,

Flicks through the TV channels,
Snatches forty winks,
Leaps out of bed . . .

John Coldwell

doing the washing

me and Mum
we play this game
with clothes,
you have to take it in turns,
she gets them clean
I get them dirty
she gets them clean
I get them dirty
she gets them clean
I get them dirty.
Mum says,
Dad's turn.

Danielle Sensier

Stepmother

Life with her is a fairy tale
She's not like any other
Totally ace and magically cool
My wicked stepmother

Paul Cookson

Being Trees

'Why not play at being trees?' asks
mum. 'Great fun.' So we try and try,
pushing branches sky-high, Jack and I.

He's an English oak, I'm a conker tree:
sparrows and starlings perch while
squirrels search in either Jack or me.

Roots spread out, dig deep,
deep down, 'Remember,' mum
says, 'trees seldom make a sound.'

Swaying, slowly swaying,
whispering, in a summer breeze . . .

Five-minutes'-worth of calm and peace.

'I'm sure that you're both growing leaves!'
Mum really likes us being trees.

Mike Johnson

I Remember

I remember
just yesterday when
I fell out of our tree
and ruined my trainers
I thought you'd go bonkers
but you just smiled
patched up my scratches.

I remember last week
when a terrible nightmare
ripped up my sleep
into long ragged curtains
that flapped at my window
like broken wings
I woke up shouting
you gave me a cuddle
and it all went away.

I remember
my first day at school
on a prairie of tarmac
the wind throwing handfuls
of rain in my face
I started to cry
and you showed me how
to play in the sandpit
and make lots of friends.

I don't remember
the long nights you sat up
when I had a fever
or a face full of spots
long, racking coughs
sweat dripping like water
from my hot red face.

I don't remember
all the lessons you taught me
how to walk, how to talk
how to grow up
and become a person.

So, today I'll remember
all these things I remember
all these things I've forgotten
how to remember
wrap them all up
into one golden parcel
just to say thank you
for being my Mum.

David Harmer

Kenning

Hand holder
Clothes folder
Cuddle maker
Cake baker
Story reader
Child feeder
Knee mender
Love sender
Mum

Daphne Kitching

Mummy's mummy

Nanna has the clean smell of ironing.
She irons a lot. Even wrinkles in socks.

Sometimes she smells buttery and sweet
which means she's been baking.
If she winks, it's a chocolate cake.
She says cakes out of shops are a cheat:
you can't taste the eggs or anything much.

In the spring she grows flowers
from little black seeds she sprinkles in pots
then she talks to them, stroking the leaves as
    they grow
so her fingers smell green like grass that's
    been cut.

When she kisses me she squeezes my cheeks
with hands that smell softly of coconut.
It's a safe, quiet, smiley smell
I remember
even when I'm not with her.

Lynne Taylor

A Message for Mother's Day

Mum, Mom, Mama,
Mother, Mater, Amma,
Mummy, Mommy, Ma,
Mother mine, in every tongue,
Yours the praises the world has sung.
So I have only this to say:
I love you now and every day.

Debjani Chatterjee

A Card for Me Mom

It is Mother's Day tomorrow
and the shops are full of wonderful things –
candles, picture-frames, pot-pourri in glass
    dishes,
but I only have money for a card, and there are
    dozens –
cards with teddies and roses, cards with moms
in dresses, with gold and red hair and blue eyes.
None of them look like me Mom.
If there was just one card to show
Mom with her gold necklace, bangles and
    earrings,
reminding me of her soft jingle-jangle as she
    washes
the curry pots or mixes the dough for rotis and
    nans,
in her silk kameezes and chiffon chunnies –
    one mom
with long black hair and flashing dark eyes
who looks more like me Mom!

Bashabi Fraser

Mothers

They're tender, caressing,
And gentle as doves
With hearts overflowing
With kindness and love;
Forgiving, forbearing,
And utterly blessed
In the steadfast belief
That they *always* know best!

Cynthia Rider

Love Me Mum

Love me
Even though I sulk for days.
Love me
Even when I answer back.
Love me
Even when I get in trouble.
Love me Mum
For I love you.

I love you
Even when I rant and rave.
I love you
Even when I'm in a mood.
I love you
Even when I'm nagging on.
I love you
For I'm your mum.

Brenda Williams

Wanted

Wanted
Someone to clean out the hamster
Twice, or three times, every week.
Someone who'll find the best places
For games of hide-and-seek.
Someone who'll stand on
    the touchline
And cheer on a cold
    Sunday morning,
Who'll welcome a friend
    home for tea
And produce extra meals
    with no warning.

Someone who'll be there for sports day
And take part in the parents' race,
Who *never* would spit on a hanky
Then use it to wipe a child's face.
Someone to pick up stray clothing
From staircase and sofa and floor,
Who'll wash it again, uncomplaining,
Or tidy it into a drawer.
Someone with kisses at bedtime,
But never in front of a friend.
Someone to act as a chauffeur.
Someone with money to lend.
Someone who'll honour a promise,
Be available, day and night.
Someone to trust with a secret.
Someone who'll make it all right.

If you're looking for job satisfaction,
A job that puts love to the test,
A job whose rewards might be hidden,
This job is one of the best.

Fiona Coward

Hushabye

Hush little baby, don't you cry
I'm going to buy you a chunk of sky
The sky over fields where the sky is blue
The sheep say baa and the cows say moo

Hush little baby, don't you cry
I'm going to buy you a chunk of sky
The sky over jungles, falling through the trees
The sky over beautiful birds and leaves

Hush little baby, don't you cry
I'm going to buy you a chunk of sky
The sky over cities where the sun shines in
To bless the cot that you lie in

Colette Sensier

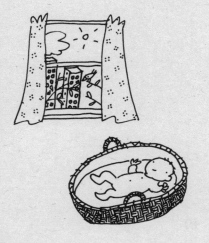

My mum is a Viking

My mum's a Viking
she wears a hat with some horns
and she has some silver swords
and she has a rounded shield
and it has a dragon on the front
and she gives me Viking stew.
She's the scariest
mum in the world because she's so strong.

Nathan Packham

Bring and Buy

Sold my mother at the Summer Fayre
to a year 3 kid. Good buy.
Six quid. A snip at half the price.
Didn't think twice, I swear.
Found a cool one, going spare
who swore, pink hair, big boots.
So brought her back to mine; arms linked.
Each footstep fell in sync.

Dined on takeaways, lay in bed
but fed-up quick with fast food,
mess and being late for Miss,
took *her* away instead.
Swapped her for another mother.
This time smarter: slick
side-parting, high-heeled shoes, posh skirt.
Looked like an advert. Tricked.

Should have guessed the rest: the muesli,
star charts, manners, tests,
in bed by eight and no buts. Please,
she's got to leave. Can't wait.
Then met my old mum. Good as new
and maybe better. Told that kid
in year 3, when he's through
I'd pay out a tenner to get her.

                            Rachel Rooney

Mums rule

Ma		Ma	Ma		Ma
Madre	Mum	Mum	Mutti	Mum	Mum
Maman	Ma	Mama	Mère		Mère
Mother		Mother	Mama		Mama
Mamma		Moeder	Ma	Mother	Ma
Mummy		Mummy	Mummy		Mam
Mother		Mother	Mother		

```
Ma                    Ma              Mum
Madre  Mum  Mum  Mutti      Mom        Mother
Maman      Ma      Mama     Mam
Mother          Mother         Maman    Madre
Mamma           Moeder                  Mama
Mummy           Mummy       Ma         Mutti
Mother          Mother         Mum   Mother
```

loved all over the world

Catharine Boddy

Mum

My mum is a woolly, soft cardigan.
She's an endless summer's day
    with a clear blue sky,
sometimes a tall clock whose fingers say,
    'Time for sleep.'
        She's a bedtime story in front
          of the fire,
    a soothing plaster,
    a tube of antiseptic cream.
    She's a flower bed full of
        sweet-smelling roses,
    a bath of pink bubbles.

Chris Ogden

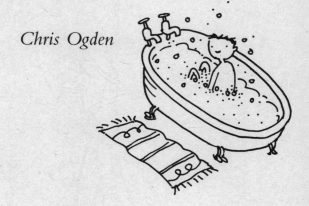

48

She's the One

She knows just what's going on
    Her memory's fantastic
Her eyes can see round corners
    She got arms made of elastic!

So many pairs of hands
    She's everywhere at once
She can tell you where your kit is
    While ironing your pants.

While she's cooking dinner
    And making shopping lists
She knows what homework's not been done
    And who your sister kissed!

She's knows what you are up to
    Wherever you may go
Don't try to get away with it
    Cos SuperMum will know!

Trevor Millum

Pantomime

(Mum is juggling baby and baking trays)
I'm going out to play
No you're not
Yes I am
Where's your sister?
She's behind you
No she's not
Yes she is
There you are, tea's ready now
We're going to play

No you're not
Yes we are
I won't say it again
What won't you say?
What I just said
What did you say?
You're not going out
You said it again
(And Mum, driven crazy, throws the custard pie)

Dave Calder

My Mum

My mum makes cakes
My mum sews clothes
My mum mends stuff
My mum is good at
Masses of things

Under the stairs there's
Underwear for mending
Upholstery for curtaining
Undercoat for painting
Under the bed there's
Uniforms for washing
Undisturbed fluff for vacuuming
Umpteen things to do, but still

My mum kicks footballs
My mum feeds ducks
My mum runs races, so
My mum's the best!

Suzanne Elvidge

Mum Used Pritt Stick

Mum used Pritt Stick
Instead of lipstick
Then went and kissed my dad

Two days passed
Both stuck fast
The longest snog they ever had.

Paul Cookson

My Mums Wears a Jelly Bra

My Mum wears a jelly bra.
She says it helps her figure.
I reckon she has matching pants
That make her bottom quiver.

Karen Costello-McFeat

Doubly My Ma

My Ma's love is a warm blanket
with the softest cosiest fleece.
I like to snuggle beside her
and shut tired eyes in peace.

Dida's love is doubly rich
because she is my Ma's Ma.
When she hugs and kisses me
I am a maharaja.

Debjani Chatterjee

Mystery Star

She makes you want to dance and shout,
She makes you want to shake about;
She makes you want to wiggle your bum,
Only joking – it's just my mum.

Naomi Seed (11)

Interfauna

It was Mother's Day
So I went down to
Interfauna
And bought
A lovely bunch of red rhinos
Mmmm,
I'd better get her
A bigger vase too.

Andy Seed

Magic

She puts her hands in the sink – with each deft
  flick
another plate comes out clean – I can't
  understand this:
even saucers are awkward to me, take an age to
  wash.
It's the same with flour: what runs and jumps
  from me
obeys her instantly, rolling itself into a neat ball
to unfurl like a handkerchief beneath her wand.
She says to the fire – go on, you, burn! – and it
  does.
Wool turns to clothes between her clicking
  fingers.
The hands are always moving, you seldom see the
  trick
till later, with surprise, you find the world
  changed:
the dust gone, the dress ironed, the food laid out
  to eat.
Clear up your things – she says – they won't put
  themselves away;

but I think if she told them to, they would.
    She's so good
at that sort of magic.

Dave Calder

Dear Mum

While you were out
A cup went and broke itself on purpose.

     A crack appeared in that old blue
       vase your great grandad
     Got from Mr Ming.
     Somehow without me even turning
       on the tap
     The sink mysteriously overflowed.
A strange jam-stain, about the size of my hand,
Suddenly appeared on the kitchen wall.
I don't think we'll ever discover exactly how
    the cat
Managed to turn on the washing machine
(Specially from the inside)
Or how Sis's pet rabbit went
    and mistook
The waste-disposal unit for
    a burrow.

I can tell you, I was really scared when, as if by
   magic,
A series of muddy footprints appeared on your
   new white carpet.
Also, I know the canary looks grubby,
But it took ages and ages
Getting it out of the vacuum-cleaner
I was being good (honest)
But I think the house is haunted so,
Knowing you're going to have a fit,
I've gone over to Gran's to lie low for a bit.

Brian Patten

Eternal Mum of the Beige-less Kind

A slash of lippy
No sign of beige
Embracing plump
Bouts of vague

Occasionally wise
A glint of wit
Rarely cries
Doesn't knit

Refuses to cook
For more than nine
Never irons
Or watches time

Doesn't say should
Ought or must
Won't own cats
Laughs at dust

Scoffs at bullies
Rejects bluff
Dances to Coldplay
In the buff

Says No to
Sanctimonious twaddle
Makes growing old
Look a doddle

Katharine Crossley

Musical Musing

Just for once
I'd love to hear it –
Music to the ear –

Mother shouting,
'Turn that racket
UP
So I can *hear*!'

Graham Denton

Fostered

She was a mother to me,
the loveliest there ever could be
was Joey.

I wasn't her own,
she had none, I was sort of on loan
to Joey.

But the time that we shared
was great, for she cared,
did Joey.

And all through my childhood
I learned what a child should
from Joey.

I learned respect for all creatures
from this kindest of teachers,
dear Joey.

Now I am called Mum
and I've tried hard to become
like Joey, my Joey.

Catherine Benson

All Right, Mum?

I do like your dress, Mum,
it's trendy, and it's cool,
but I'd wear jeans, if I were you,
to meet me from school.

Can you come in Dad's car?
It's not that yours is bad,
but the stickers in the windows
are a bit sad.

I love the way you've done your hair,
but I should wear a scarf.
No, *I* don't think it's funny,
but my friends might laugh.

Your make-up rather suits you.
You know I'm really glad
my best friend told me yesterday
that I look like my dad.

Of course I'm really proud of you.
I'm not at all ashamed,
and if they ask, 'Whose mother's that?'
I can't be blamed.

Celia Warren

One to one

all my friends have
a mum and dad
or mum and stepdad
or dad and stepmum
or mum and her boyfriend
or dad and his girlfriend

I just have my mum
the best friend I've ever had

Lynne Taylor

Supermum to the rescue

My mum flies in
the air her hair
behind her. She lifts
a bit of building
and throws it
at the robbers and the robbers say
ouch

Tom Armes

A greengage is a type of plum

A greengage is a type of plum
I know this fact because my mum
brought home a sack full of the stuff.
'Well you can never have enough
of fresh fruit for the family,'
she said, 'especially when it's free.'
That night we ate them ripe and raw.
Then, finding there were plenty more,
decided that she ought to try
a recipe for greengage pie.
And as the sack was hardly dented
other puddings she invented.
Crumble, jams and roly-poly
bakes and cakes were served up solely
for our pleasure. But no thanks
were given from her hungry ranks.
Worse than this, we soon grew tired
of the taste, once quite admired.
On day eight to our displeasure
after dinner, in great measure,
we received, against our wishes,
stewed greengages served in dishes.

My father, not a man to grumble,
was overheard to softly mumble,
'Oh no, it's not those things again.'
My mother didn't answer – Then
stood up and, walking to his chair,
she raised his serving in the air
and calmly without warning tipped
it from above. The warm plums dripped
all sweet and sticky from his brow,
upon the table, dishless now.
Mum returned back to her seating
and resumed her silent eating.
Dad went to wash, while leaving us
to eat our pudding without fuss.

There is no moral to this tale
of greed or gratitude or scale.
These things apply, but my point is
that I'll remember in a quiz
this fructal fact (all thanks to mum):
A greengage is a type of plum.

Rachel Rooney

Mummy

Is helpful
Plays with me
Likes to eat chocolate

Mum

Mummy
She's beautiful
She cuddles me
She does kind things

Oliver Lowe (6)

Victoria's Poem

Send me upstairs without any tea,
refuse me a plaster to stick on my knee.

Make me kiss Grandpa who smells of his pipe,
make me eat beetroot, make me eat tripe.

Throw all my best dolls into the river.
Make me eat bacon and onions – with liver.

Tell Mr Allan I've been a bad girl,
rename me Nellie, rename me Pearl.

But don't, even if
the world suddenly ends,
   ever again,
      Mother,
wipe my face with a tissue
in front of my friends.

Fred Sedgwick

She Is

She is one who always takes my side,
She is my friend, philosopher and guide.
She rebukes but with love in the heart,
She gives that push to make a good start.
She weeds the misfortunes whenever they crop,
She knows where to start and where to stop.
I'd never go anywhere but be with her rather,
Cos she is no one other than my MOTHER.

Nivedita Bhattacharjee

Skateboard Surprise
(A tanka)

Dad fell off at once
Sister lasted down the path
Thought I was the best
Till mum went round the block twice
Balanced on her hands

Paul Cookson

My Musical Mother

My mother loves to sing.
She sings whenever and wherever.
Like, in supermarkets,
I'll stand and cringe, while
She la-la-las her way down every aisle,
And I'll pretend we're not together.
Only, it doesn't seem to work:
People smile at me, or smirk,
And then I cringe some more.

She sings
When she's hanging clothes out
On the line; and when she's making tea
There she'll be: joining in
With whoever's on the radio (although
She often doesn't know
The words). Trust me
To have a mother who's so musical –

Still,

I wouldn't change her,
Not for anything –
Because (and whisper this bit quietly)
I love to hear my mother sing.

Gillian Floyd

In my Mum's handbag...

Six half-used lipsticks,
Four money-off coupons for chicken nuggets,
Tissues, tissues, tissues.
A comb,
Half a comb,
Some teeth from a comb.

A fat purse,
Three old lottery tickets,
A black glove,
A green glove,
Crushed crisps,
That bun I couldn't eat
At Auntie Mabel's.
Daisy's old dummy,
Biscuits for the bulldog
At number forty-two,
A scrunched-up message
Saying, Yow ar speshul
(From me – years ago).
Ten aspirins,
Two cocktail sausages –
And that letter from
My teacher that we couldn't find
Anywhere!

Rita Ray

Space Poems

Chosen by
Gaby Morgan

Blast off into outer space with this brilliant collection
of poems about stars, rockets, space explorers,
planets, aliens and the moon.

Space Counting Rhyme

10 flying saucers, 10 flashing lights
9 glowing trails, 9 meteorites
8 silver spaceships trying to find
7 lost aliens left behind
6 burning comets blazing fire
5 red rockets blasting higher
4 satellites, 4 radar dishes
3 stars shooting means 3 wishes
2 bright lights – the moon and sun
1 little me to shine upon

Paul Cookson